Jenny Jellyfish

HAPPY READING!

This book is especially for:

_____

Suzanne Tate
Author—
brings fun and
facts to us in her
Nature Series.

James Melvin
Illustrator—
brings joyous life
to Suzanne Tate's
characters.

Author Suzanne Tate
and
Illustrator James Melvin

Jenny Jellyfish

A Tale of Wiggly Jellies

Suzanne Tate

Illustrated by James Melvin

Nags Head Art

To Lucy Willis
who gave boundless love
to her students for 51 years

Library of Congress Catalog Card Number 00-92755
ISBN 978-1-878405-30-2
ISBN 1-878405-30-6
Published by
Nags Head Art, Inc., P.O. Box 2149, Manteo, NC 27954
Copyright © 2001 by Nags Head Art, Inc.
Revised 2005

Jenny Jellyfish was a Moon Jelly—
floating free in the sea like a tiny moon.
She was a beauty! You could see pink and
pretty colors on her clear, bell-like body.

Jenny's friends were floating in the water around her.
Each one was a Moon Jelly—an animal
with no heart, brains or bones!

Jenny Jellyfish had so many friends
she couldn't even name them all!
Johnny, Jerry, Jackie, and Jiggly Jelly
were just a few of Jenny's friends.

The Moon Jellies drifted together
and were often pulled by the water.
But each jellyfish could also move itself
by squeezing its body back and forth.

Jenny and her friends were almost all water themselves—wiggly and jiggly animals. Jiggly Jelly was Jenny's best friend and the wiggliest one of all.

He would wiggle and jiggle—just to show off!

Most of the jellies would laugh at Jiggly
as they drifted and moved in the sea.

But Jenny Jellyfish worried about him.
"Why can't you be still?" she asked.
Jiggly didn't listen and kept on wiggling.

One day, Crabby was swimming in the sea.
He saw Jiggly wiggling away.
"I'll swim up under that jellyfish,"
he thought to himself.
"It will be a good place to hide."

But a big sea turtle had spied a meal
in that wiggly, jiggly jellyfish!
Crabby saw the big creature
just in time and scooted away!

The turtle turned and tried to catch
Crabby instead of Jiggly!

But Crabby quickly hid in an old bucket
lying on the bottom of the sea.
He was surprised to find Nabby there.

"What's going on?" she asked.
"A big turtle would rather eat me than
a jellyfish," he replied.

Meanwhile, Jenny scolded Jiggly as they floated in the sea. "If you weren't so wiggly, the turtles wouldn't notice you," she told him.

Jiggly didn't want to listen. But he watched as Jenny fired tiny stingers from her tentacles. She soon grabbed a little fish that was stunned by the poison in her stings.

Jiggly thought, "That's too much trouble.
I'll just grab tiny eggs and animals
from the water that flows over me."

Right away, he began to slurp up plankton
with his thick mouth tentacles.

As Jenny and Jiggly and their friends drifted and ate, more and more jellies joined them.
"There must be hundreds of jellyfish here now," Jenny said. "We look like a floating raft of jelly."

Soon, female jellyfish like Jenny began dropping eggs. Jiggly and the other males released a liquid that fertilized the eggs.

Baby Moon Jellies began to hatch and
hang onto the adults' tentacles.
The jelly babies were as tiny as a pencil dot.

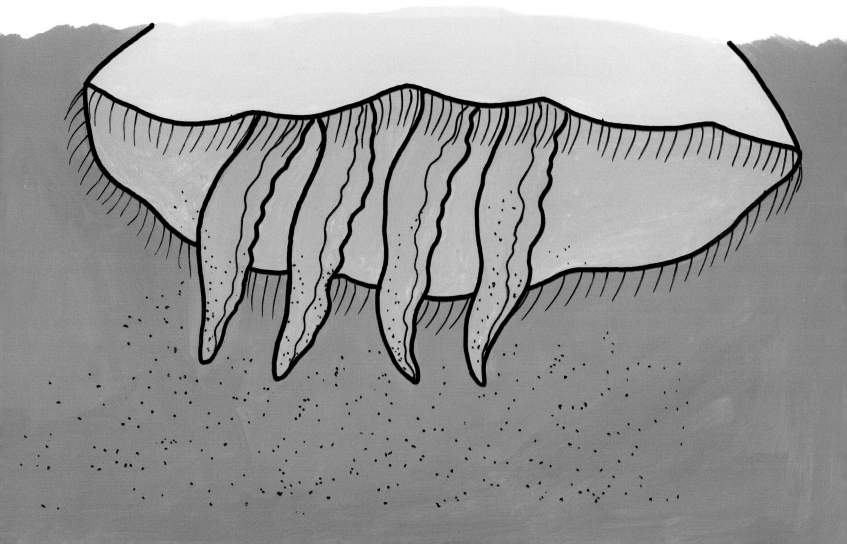

The tiny jellies soon dropped down to the bottom
and grabbed hold of oysters and rocks.
There, they grew and became tube-like
animals called polyps.

The polyps then formed many buds that popped off
— and became new jellyfish!

Later, Jiggly was looking for Jenny.
But he couldn't find her anywhere!
There were so many jellies in the water.

A rainbow spot on some clouds was
beginning to show in the sky.
It was called a "sun dog."

Jiggly saw the "sun dog" and worried.
"That's a sign of bad weather," he thought.
"The wind will likely blow and blow."

The wind did begin to howl.
And strong waves bounced
the raft of Moon Jellies.
Those watery animals were helpless!

The big waves washed them closer
and closer to the sandy beach.
Suddenly, the Moon Jellies were
piled up on it—a bunch of watery blobs!

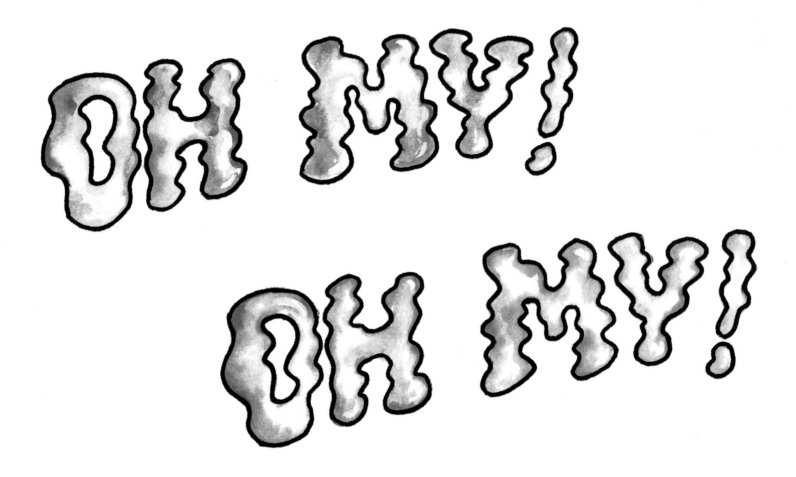

It was Jenny—not hurt—but scared!

Jiggly—who was nearby—couldn't even wiggle.
For the wind was dry, and the sun was hot.
"We need water!" Jenny cried.
"Maybe HELPFUL HUMANS will find us,"
Jiggly said hopefully.

Soon, a family of HUMANS came along,
looking for shells after the storm.
They were surprised to see so many jellyfish
piled up on the beach.

"Let's be HELPFUL HUMANS," the woman said.
"We can try to keep the jellyfish wet until
the tide brings high water to the beach."

"Here's my first bucketful," said the little girl.
"I'll help too," her brother said. "These are
Moon Jellies—they won't sting us like other jellyfish."

More HELPFUL HUMANS came along
and splashed water on the Moon Jellies too.
At last, the tide came in and lifted up
all the jellies from the beach.

Jiggly couldn't help wiggling for joy!
This time, Jenny didn't scold him.
"I feel wiggly too," Jenny sighed happily.
"Thanks to HELPFUL HUMANS,
we can float free in the sea once more."